Honest, short and to the point answers about the MLM/Networking Marketing Industry?

Let's Be Honest about MLM/Network Marketing

MLM Fundamentals

Dr. H.L. Barner
"A Buk an Hour Gives Power"

Finally, a "buk" that honestly answer questions about MLM/Network Marketing businesses. This amazing buk address many of the concerns and rumors about this industry and will inspire you to join or be glad you didn't. In either case you will get plenty of facts that will help you make an informed decision.

LET'S BE HONEST ABOUT MLM/NETWORK MARKETING
MLM FUNDAMENTALS

Copyright © 2014 H. L. Barner.

All rights reserved. No part of this book may be used or reproduced by any means, graphic, electronic, or mechanical, including photocopying, recording, taping or by any information storage retrieval system without the written permission of the publisher except in the case of brief quotations embodied in critical articles and reviews.

iUniverse books may be ordered through booksellers or by contacting:

iUniverse LLC
1663 Liberty Drive
Bloomington, IN 47403
www.iuniverse.com
1-800-Authors (1-800-288-4677)

Because of the dynamic nature of the Internet, any web addresses or links contained in this book may have changed since publication and may no longer be valid. The views expressed in this work are solely those of the author and do not necessarily reflect the views of the publisher, and the publisher hereby disclaims any responsibility for them.

Any people depicted in stock imagery provided by Thinkstock are models, and such images are being used for illustrative purposes only.
Certain stock imagery © Thinkstock.

ISBN: 978-1-4917-4191-7 (sc)
ISBN: 978-1-4917-4192-4 (e)

Library of Congress Control Number: 2014913111

Printed in the United States of America.

iUniverse rev. date: 09/08/2014

Contents

Bottom Line Up Front (BLUF) vii
Dedication ix
Foreword xi

Episode 1:   My Story I am so glad I was introduced to MLM 1
Episode 2:   Network Marketing vs Multi-Level Marketing 7
Episode 3:   Are You in the Orange Business? 18
Episode 4:   Everyone Sells 24
Episode 5:   Traditional Businesses versus MLM 34
Episode 6:   A Divine Beginning 57
Episode 7:   Why not a Job? 65
Episode 8:   Why not a Traditional Business? 73
Episode 9:   Can You Really Earn Money in MLM? 81

Episode 10: What about Tax Benefits?...... 86
Episode 11: Is This a Family Business?...... 96
Episode 12: Is it Difficult to Work a
             MLM Business?...................... 103
Episode 13: Who are Owners of
             MLM Businesses?...................110

Recommendations...115
Epic..117
Acknowledgments 119
Backup 127
About the Author...131

Bottom Line Up Front (BLUF)

Why so many people are starting a MLM home business? Good question! Simply because of the following:

- Great Tax Benefits
- Low cost & low risk
- Unlimited income potential
- No educational requirements
- Great products & services
- Anyone can do it
- BIG fun
- Exciting
- Meet lots of people from around the country and world
- Everyone should own a business – this is the American Dream
- It is legal, ethical, and moral
- Lots of help, training, and support

- You are in it for yourself but not by yourself
- It does take consistent work
- People do quit and some never get started
- There are ups and downs
- People will get on your nerve
- You will get rejections, broken appointments, and NOs
- It makes SENSE and I am just being HONEST

Dedication

I first dedicate this buk to my Lord and Savior Jesus Christ for blessing me with this gift and idea.

I dedicate this buk to all the people who are considering joining the Multi-level-Marketing family. I know you will be amazed and extremely successful if you are willing and committed to helping others achieve their dreams and goals and if you treat each and every opportunity as a business, respect the other network marketing companies, be honest in your presentations, sincere with your support, put God first, family second, and never sacrifice integrity for success.

Foreword

Let's start with this: Everyone has an opinion! Most of the books written about network marketing and multi-level marketing (MLM) are very good and provide new entrepreneurs with a good foundation on how to start their home business. However, it is important to note that many of the authors of these books have little or no personal experience in the business. Therefore, they must rely on interviews, consulting other books, observations, small business principles, and a little guesswork. You will find out that most of the better and more accurate books are written by individuals who have spent years developing expertise and knowledge through training and building a large successful network marketing business. If you discover some conflicting information in this buk versus what you may have read in other books it is due to my more than 38 years of professional Multi-Level-Marketing (MLM)/Network Marketing experience.

Since 1976 I have attended hundreds of training events, seminars, rallies, and conventions. I consistently plug into conference calls, webinars, and follow facebook, twitter and surf the internet. I have built national and international downline organizations with multiple MLM/Network Marketing companies achieving their top income levels, recruiting awards and recognition. I have personally trained and mentor thousands of MLM/Network Marketers throughout the United States, Canada, England, & Germany. I have help thousands of people start MLM home businesses earning thousands of dollars.

As a master recruiter and presenter I have done thousands of business presentations all around the world. I have been the featured and keynote speaker from the local hotel meetings and company conventions to the Queen Elizabeth Conference in England. I have read and collected a huge number of some of the best MLM and motivational books ever written. I have a library of information on present and past MLM companies, their training materials, video, cassette tapes, VHS videos, and much more. This is my profession, passion, and calling in life.

A special note from the Author and Founder of "Buks".

Now, you may be wondering why this is called a 'buk' versus book. Well, it is quite simple. We live in a very fast paced society and need accurate information quickly. I have decided to publish 'buks' that are designed to give you the information you are looking for without all the bells and whistles. Don't get me wrong;

there are thousands of great books that are worthy of your time; However, time is money. Therefore, you must manage your time by seeking resources that provide exactly what you need when you need it. My buks are designed to give you this information in a format that can be read and understood within in an hour or two. Simply put, Barner's buks are short books: A Buk an Hour Gives Power! There you have it! This is the very first "buk" ever published.

Episode I

My Story I am so glad I was introduced to MLM

It was the fall of 1975. I had just completed the most difficult experience of my young life: United States Army Basic Training. It was a tremendous and wonderful experience that also made me question my sanity when I enlisted! However, I would not change a thing if I had to do it all again because it put me on a journey that changed my life forever.

Months after arriving at Fort Eustis, Virginia, for my first permanent duty station I enrolled in some college courses. My goal was to complete my bachelor's degree around the same time my fiancee (and now wife Fran) was scheduled to graduate from college. We had been dating since high school and had always talked about staying together forever. Our parents, though, made us promise that we wouldn't marry until we graduated from college and started our careers. You can understand why I was motivated to earn my degree. Within 12 months, I had completed my associate degree and started taking courses toward earning a bachelor's degree while also excelling in my military duties. A reporter for the installation's newspaper took note of my accomplishments and asked for an interview. The title of the article she wrote was "A Soldier and his dreams." The article was picked up by the local newspaper. Within a few days of that article being published I began receiving phone calls about business opportunities. The first call came from a dude in the Air Force. I don't remember his name or anything about him, but I do remember going to his home to learn about the opportunity. This was my first exposure to networking market. I didn't have a clue about the industry, but the concept caught my attention. I told the guy I had to "think" about it.

I was continuing to receive phone calls from all these people I did not know. I began to get a little worried because I had no idea what was going on with all these strange folks calling me and inviting me to their homes to talk about a business opportunity. Keep in mind that there were no cell phones back then. These folks were calling my workplace and I was getting messages from the admin office. One day I received message from another Air Force dude, Captain Hector New. I decided to call him back to see what he was offering. To tell the truth, I was hoping someone was calling to give me a cash award or something! Anyway, Captain New invited me to another home meeting. He explained how he was impressed with the article and felt that I could go far in his business. He lived in a very lovely home and his family was extremely nice. His wife, Rose, was the most exciting and enthusiastic woman I had ever met. After the meeting I spoke with the News and told them I wanted to join. Needless to say, it was one of the best decisions of my life and I hope that by the end of this buk you will be just as excited to join me in this life changing industry!

One other thing I want to mention to you upfront is that I will repeat myself throughout my buks because I believe that some things are worth repeating and I want to make sure you understand the things that you really must wrap your mind around. So when you notice that I have repeated myself you may want to highlight or underline it. Some of the things may not seem important but as you read my other buks you will see what I am talking about. Oh, one final thing! I will not be reference what other people have said. The information that follows comes from my 38 years of personal and professional experience working with thousands of people, products and non product based companies, testing and experimenting with different MLM/Networking systems, strategies, and let's try this and see what happens approach also. And yes I have read the majority to the books written about our industry and to be honest most of them are excellent. So don't look for a bunch of footnotes, appendix, glossary, bibliographies and source notes. However, I will list several of my favorite MLM & Motivational books in the back of this buk. Now get busy my friend. Thanks for your attention.

Your Notes:
Why do you need to start now?

_____
_____
_____
_____
_____
_____
_____
_____
_____
_____
_____
_____
_____
_____
_____
_____
_____

Episode II

Network Marketing vs Multi-Level Marketing

What is the difference?

Several "expert or professional" networking marketers believe that multi-level marketing (MLM) and network marketing are synonymous. Some even believe that the two are just different types of marketing strategies but in theory the same.

This is close to being correct, but not exactly right. Allow me to set the record straight for once and for all with the hope of getting everyone on the same sheet of music. Network marketing is an industry and MLM is a strategy in the industry. In other words, multi-level marketing is one of two ways in which products and services are delivered to the consumer within the network marketing industry.

Let's use the transportation industry as a metaphor to help explain what I mean. Best Fruits is a distribution company based in Florida. They ship oranges, peaches, apples, bananas, and other fruits all over the entire United States. Best Fruits relies on the transportation industry to move its products daily! Depending on where the fruit is being sent, Best Fruits uses one of the following forms of transportation to get the fruit to the customers while it is fresh and ripe: trucks, cars, boats, trains, or airplanes. Of course, there are many other forms of transportation; however, the main point is to understand that within the transportation industry there are many vehicles by which to transport products.

Now let us see how the transportation industry parallels with network marketing. Network marketing is a face-to-face form of promoting/selling products and services. Network marketing is the industry and within this industry there are two forms of distrubtion: direct sales and multi-level marketing.

Direct sales is probably the most recognized, acceptable, and widely used form of selling and marketing products and services. The most important aspects of direct sales are two-fold: selling and commissions.

In direct sales you must become a highly trained, skilled, knowledgeable and professional sales person. Most people in direct sales sell extremely expensive products and services, therefore, they require an extensive amount of knowledge. The products and services that use direct sales include automobiles, life insurance, large appliances, furniture, real estate, stocks, and much more. In most cases, the consumer becomes convinced (sold) on the idea that they should buy something that will normally create a debt that will last for years. Direct sales people must be skillful in convincing others to buy things they may or may not need. Since the invention of the credit card, sales people get consumers to spend money they do not have. They are relentless, confident, focused, determined, highly trained, and prepared for rejection. Their drive and charisma will draw people in until that "No" turns into a "Yes." However, we need direct sales people and they need us. Sales is what makes the economy grow and as someone once said "Sales makes the world go round."

Why are they so aggressive (so good at what they do)? They are highly trained professionals who take their skills and abilities very seriously. We depend on their knowledge of the product/service in order to make immediate decisions. People in MLM can learn a lot from direct sales people. Years ago, direct sales people got a lot of bad press due to a few dishonest sales people. Just like any industry there are always a few bad apples in the bunch. Today, you don't hear very much about dishonest sales people because if they are dishonest, bad news travel fast. With a push of a button on your smart phone or laptop hundreds of people can learn about your bad experience with a company or sales person. Keep in mind that MLM representatives are in the same boat. If you provide bad information, people can hear about it quickly.

Another reason direct sales people are so aggressive with their sales techniques is because they only earn their money from closing the deal. Some sales people may receive a base salary and a bonus for reaching a certain sale amount, but others are paid strictly on commission—they don't make a penny if they don't sell something. Unlike the different types of leadership bonuses, fast start bonuses, and

<u>the residual income MLM representatives earn,</u> direct sales people (with a few exceptions) earn no income until the next sale. Thus, they must be good at what they do, know their products, and close each sale. If the direct sales person is good, the sky is the limit on how much money they can make! It is possible to earn millions of dollars and have a very comfortable and secure lifestyle as a direct sales person. However, it can be a very stressful, time consuming, and even an expensive career. The sales person must be willing to invest in training, seminars, product meetings, etc. Some direct sales people have to invest in expensive inventory without any guarantees that they will get their money back. Often times, it becomes a dog-eat-dog world. You will find that these folks rarely share information, techniques, ideas, or offer support to each other. You can find the same type of behavior in the MLM side as well. Neither side is perfect, but each is doing better than in the past.

Multi-level marketing does not require any special skills, education, training, business background, or technical training. Product knowledge is minimal and the company whose products or service you are marketing will probably provide you with the information you may need. These products are normally quite inexpensive, but are of very good quality. Most of these products can be purchased at the local mall. MLM customers are normally using some form of that product already and have product knowledge. In many cases, the customer may know more about the benefits of a particular product than you do. Because the products or services are so affordable, you don't have to sell them! Multi-level marketers *promote* products and services of different companies. We merely ask people (friends, relatives, and associates) to do for us what they are already doing for someone else. These folks tend to be very loyal customers, and there is nothing better for a company than having loyal customers who purchase their products and services each and every month.

Companies can provide consumers with lower priced products or services while maintaining high quality and they enjoy tremendous savings due to low or no advertising budget. MLM is a relationship-oriented type of business that relies on referrals and loyalty from their customers. This is one of the key reasons why companies use the MLM strategy to move their products from Wall Street to Main Street.

Additionally, MLMers are not required to promote large numbers of products or services. Their success is contingent upon their ability to recruit and teach others to promote the products or services to their friends. Therefore, simplicity is the key to duplication and duplication is the key to rapid and exponential growth.

Another major difference between direct sales and MLM is that with MLM you have the opportunity to get paid for your efforts *and* from the efforts of the people you have recruited (often referred to as your downline). This is probably the most important factor that separates MLM from direct sales. An MLMer can build an organization of people who will duplicate his or her efforts by sharing the income opportunity with others to join this industry and become MLMers. Multi-level marketers receive training and support throughout their career with the person who introduced the opportunity to them (the sponsor). A sponsor is not the "boss," nor is the sponsor smarter, better, or even wealthier than you. This is just the person who introduced you to that particular company and opportunity. To continue with the process these new folks on your team will start building their business by asking their family and friends to become customers and also offer the income opporutnity by joining the team. If you continue to help new MLMers start their business, you will receive residual income and overrides in the form of bonuses for working with and training your new business partners.

As you can see, MLM is drastically different from direct sales even though they are the same industry with the same purpose in mind -- to make money.

> Remember, you can transport as many products and services as you desire. Technology will allow you to earn income from many sources.

Your Notes:
What do you know about MLM?

_____

_____

_____

_____

_____

_____

_____

_____

_____

_____

_____

_____

_____

_____

_____

_____

_____

_____

_____

Episode III

Are You in the Orange Business?
Be an expert of the MLM/ Network Marketing industry

Meet brothers George and Earl. Both own and operate separate businesses. George is the president of B & B Trucking, a long haul-trucking business located in Portsmouth, Virginia. He has 20 16-wheeler tractor-trailers. He is in the business of transporting other companies' products throughout the United States. George has developed a solid reputation for making deliveries on time.

The other brother, Earl, lives in Florida, where he operates Earl's Fruits & Vegetables, Inc. Earl owns several orange and apple orchards as well as 100 acres of farm land where he grows a variety of vegetables. His fruits and vegetables are considered some of the best tasting in the nation. Recently, Earl called George to arrange to have some oranges transported to North Carolina. After agreeing on a price, George sent three of his trucks down to Florida to haul Earl's oranges back to North Carolina. Before they left, Earl handed George a one page document instructing George on how to care for the oranges during the trip.

During the trip back to North Carolina, George and his drivers stop at a truck stop in South Carolina to refuel the trucks and grab a bite to eat. While George was refueling his trucks a family pulled up along side one of George's trucks that happened to have a picture of sunshine-bright colored oranges. A little boy got of the minivan, walked over to George, and asked, "Are you in the orange business?" Geogre smiled and said, "No, I'm in the trucking business."

Just like George, you are not *in* company X that sells vitamins, soap, cosmetics, insurance, energy, newspaper, long distance, phone cards, or any other kind of product or service. You are in NETWORK MARKETING. I realize you must have some knowledge of your company and the products or services you are moving, but <u>you do not have to, nor should you, become an expert on the products and services of that company</u>. You must become an expert in network marketing!

DON'T BE AN EXPERT ON THE PRODUCTS OR THE COMPANY!

George did not become an expert on oranges! Sure, Earl gave him some basic instructions on how to care for the oranges during the trip; however, Earl did not bore his brother with all the details on how the trees were planted, the ways in which to grow the oranges, when to pick them, or how to select the best ones. He simply shared with George tips on making sure the oranges stayed as fresh as possible during the trip.

What George did need to have expert knowledge of was in caring for his trucks. He needed to know how to drive them, fuel them up, maintain them, and the laws associated with owning them.

Likewise, as a network marketer, you need to know what it is going to take for you to keep moving. You need to know how to hang in there (move) when you get a flat tire (rejected) or when those negative friends and family members tell you it won't work (bugs on the windshield) and cause you to lose your vision. How about when you start to run out of gas (no one signs up) or you are lost and don't have a road map (sponsor quits or you can locate your upline). Don't forget about those pot holes (dead representatives are folks you have recruited, but who aren't working the business.

Network marketing is simply advertising, promoting, and/or selling services or products mostly by word-of-mouth. What makes this so successful is the fact that most people already have the necessary skills to be successful in MLM. We make recommendations everyday. Really! We let people know about the good movie we just watched, a great book we just read, a fabulous new restaurant we just ate at...we want others to enjoy the things we have enjoyed so we tell them about it. However, we normally don't get paid for sharing these recommendations.

You are in the network marketing industry building a multi-level marketing business. You are NOT in the energy, vitamins, phone, cosmetics, or any other kind of business.

I will talk more about the above in some of my upcoming episodes or next buk. So hold on while I go and grab a bite to eat. Be back soon!

Your Notes:
What do you know about your industry?

Episode IV

Everyone Sells

GET REAL EVERYONE SELLS SOMETHING! WHAT?

As I stated earlier, the two vehicles commonly used in networking marketing are direct sales and multi-level marketing. These two methods basically determine how a sales person or representative will be paid by company X. Direct sales has been the most popular and accepted form of network marketing since humans discovered the financial power of "selling." Traditionally, in direct sales a sales person earns a salary strictly through commissions resulting from the sale of a product. No other income structure is available to these sales people. Commissions are normally quite high; the sales territory is boundaryless; and the inventory of products unlimited. Direct sales offer complete freedom to fail and as well to succeed. There is no set work day or a boss watching your every movement. Success or failure are totally based on the person's willingness to go after it day in and day out. Once the product or service is sold, that peson becomes unemployed. Think about real estate brokers. When they sell a new home, that's it. They are out of work, and some times, money, until they sell acquire and/or sell the next home. This is what drives direct sales people. They have a passion to make the next sale!

The world depends on sales people. Without them the economy will come to a complete halt. Every product and service that we use are sold to us by sales people. The sad thing is that no one seems to like people in sales. People run when they see someone in sales coming their way. In multi-level marketing your friends and family members can run, but they can't hide.

The things we take for granted. When you get up each morning from that warm, comfortable bed, put on your favorite robe and slippers, walk on the carpeted hallway down the stairs to the kitchen where you prepare a hot cup of coffee in your favorite cup, and then enjoy a plate of eggs, bacon, grits, biscuits, and a bowl of fruit, you should think about thanking sales people because they played a big part in your morning routine.

Everyone sells and we sell every day. Look at it this way. When you get dressed in the morning to go on a job interview you are preparing to sell yourself – talent, skills, looks, attitude, and desire to be a part of a team. On the weekend when you put on your finest threads (clothes) to go out on that hot date you are selling yourself. When you join a club or organization, sports team, apply for college, dating, networking with others, etc. you are selling something. Yeah, I know, you are selling yourself, but selling is selling and the only difference is how are you getting paid for doing it. Most of the time it is money without a doubt. Other times it is a new job, college degree, new friends, a girlfriend or boyfriend, an opportunity, or something as simple as a good feeling. But we sell from the day we are born until we leave this world. And if you were sold on Jesus and you bought him you will be enjoying the next world. That was good, huh?

Unfortunately, sales professionals get a bad rap and it is becoming more difficult to have a successful sales career. Just like other professions, there are too many bad apples selling bad products and providing bad customer service in the MLM business. The few always make the many look bad.

How do we promote, advertise and/or notify consumers of a new or improved product or service? Before the Internet, we used television, newspapers, billboards, posters, flyers, signs, and word-of-mouth. Word-of-mouth is the most powerful form of advertisement on the planet. Why? Because it gives the consumer something that no other form of advertising does and that is "emotion." Our society buys more products and services on impulse, which is driven by emotion, than any other country in the world. If it makes us feel good or the sales person makes us feel good, we buy it whether we need it or not. Just about every decision we make is based on emotion. (This is also why we have so many "garage sales")

Word-of-mouth advertising is still as strong today. Matter of fact, most products and services bought are based on a friend's or relative's recommendation. Believe it or not, we will even consider the recommendation of a stranger before we commit to a final purchase. MLM gives you the opportunity to continue making recommendations, but to also get paid for it.

If word-of-mouth advertising is so powerful, then why do companies use the media to promote and advertise? The number one reason is because they can reach the masses quickly! Companies know they lose that personal touch, but they simply bet on the numbers. Doing so, though, they no longer have a loyal customer base. To compensate for the loss of that personal touch, companies use "celebrities" as a substitute. Americans seem to have emotional attachments to TV stars, athletes, politicians, religious leaders, movie stars, business leaders, and others. Therefore, by using celebrity endorsements it sort of compensates for the loss of that "personal" touch. Our society watches thousands of hours of television and has become emotionally attached to the television and just about everything on it. The TV industry makes billions of dollars from commercials, and celebrities make millions in endorsements. I am willing to bet most celebrities do not use nor have ever heard of the products and services they help market.

Despite the power of television and the celebrities endorsing everything from garden hoses to make up, personal recommendations done face-to-face are still the most powerful, effective, and most rewarding form of marketing. MLM was here first and will always be the preferred method.

If the truth is to be completely told, the reason why MLM really works is because you don't really need to market to the masses to be successful. Companies that use MLM networking to market their products and services only require you to gather a small number of customers and then teach others to do the same. These companies realize that the average person starting a business with them can barely afford to pay that small fee not to mention pay for newspaper, radio, or TV ads. They bank on you getting a few customers and a few business partners and before you know it they have thousands of customers and business owners. It works and it works very well.

When I first started my MLM career I was not sure if I could sell products or services and recruit others to do the same. I thought you had to go to school and to learn how to sell. It is not easy in the sense that you have to ask people to change their buying habits to support your business. At first is really difficult because people don't like to change. But family and friends have a tendency to do just to encourage and support you. There are those friends and family members who will not and that can be very discouraging. Sometimes your closes friends and family members are the most negative group of people. Many new

MLM professionals quit before they get started because they think that if their ~~only~~ own family members will not use the products or service no one will. That is far from the truth. Again, most family and friends will eventually support you especially when they know the product or service is good and cost less or equal too what they are already using. So remember, they will come around just don't quit.

You are already equipped to be successful in MLM, so why not give it a shot?

Your Notes:
Who sells what in your community?

"Things you need to know before launching your MLM home business"

Episode V

Traditional Businesses versus MLM

EVERYONE SHOULD OWN A BUSINESS WITH MLM EVERYONE CAN

Traditional Business Model:

This system was created by man to exercise his God-given right to participate in the world of capitalism. This model is widely used in the United States under the following structures: small business, S corporation, C corporation, partnerships, LLC, and so forth.

The traditional business model was designed so that the owner determines the worth/value of the employees. Thus, your pay is determined by several factors, such as your education, special training, skills, experience, and the company's financial statement.

When determining your pay there is one thing that is for certain: you will never make more money than your boss. Remember, the pay you get will never be what you think you are worth, only what your employer (boss) thinks you are worth.

This is true because the employer has to spend a great deal of money on overhead. In a traditional business these items include: employee medical benefits, business taxes, advertising, legal representation, accountants, business insurance, worker's compensation, payroll, holiday pay, etc. The owner is also making sure there is enough income to cover his or her golf club membership, month long vacations, tailor-made clothes, boat dock fees, political donations, fund raising dinners, etc. While this may not be true of all business owners, there is no getting around the fact that the owner is well-compensated because he or she has placed their value above yours.

They will pay you just enough money to keep you from quiting and you will work just hard enough to keep them from firing you.

Traditional Businesses are the true Pyramid Companies!

What is a "pyramid" company, you ask? Well, I am glad you asked because you deserve to know the truth. Here it is: The company you work for is, in truth, a pyramid company. What? No way! Yes, way! The company you work for is more than likely a pyramid company. Check out the definition of a pyramid company: a business, corporation, or entity that has employees, makes money from their efforts, makes huge promises of promotions and benefits, and here is the biggie...you are at the bottom and will never become the CEO or be promoted to top.

By that definition it appears that most businesses/organizations use a pyramid structure to maintain control. Think about it! You will never, ever get to the top of any of these organizations. However, as long as you are there they will earn or get money from you. Laugh, cry, get mad, but this is the simple truth.

Everyone reading this buk is quite familiar with having a job. This is the American dream. Or is it? Below are examples of things that occur in our lives:

We have BIG Dreams and Ideas!
We go to school!
We get a good education!
We find a good job
We get married
We buy a car
We buy a house
We have children
We stop dreaming. We don't have time to dream; it's more like an nightmare now.

We create debt trying to keep up with the Jones

We work harder for less pay

We become unhappy

We blame our spouses, our parents, siblings, or friends for our unhappinenss

We send our children to college

We create more debt

We blame our children

We don't like our lives. We hate getting up in the morning

We get a divorce! Hopefully the grass is greener on the other side

We create more debt

We become very unhappy

We get married again oops the grass is not greener

We create more debt

We find a part-time job because we need more money and hate going home

We are really unhappy

We retire from our primary job, but start a second career

We have high blood pressure, bad cholesterol, and take antidepressants

We have our first heart attack

We wish we were young again

We forgot about our BIG DREAMS!

We work until we die

We should have started a MLM business

NO! MLM is not a Pyramid System! Network marketing is the oldest and most powerful distribution system since the beginning of time. What is it? Again, it is the advertising, promoting, and selling of products or services primarily by word-of-mouth.

Now that network marketing has been properly defined, below are the two vehicles used in this industry. Yes, I am going to repeat myself because it is so important you get this!

Direct Sales:

Most people know, understand, and accept this form of marketing. Direct sales deal with people face-to-face! Direct sales people normally sell things like luxury cars, life insurance, real estate, investments, and on a smaller scale, high-end appliances, boats, etc.. In most cases, this sales force sells things that cost a lot of money and put customers into debt.

You definitely need sales skills in order to convince someone they need something they don't or to take on 20-to-30 years of debt. These men and women are good! You have heard these expressions before that describe just these type of sales people:

"He could sell ice to an Eskimo."

"She could sell hot chocolate in the desert!"

Multi-Level Marketing:

This vehicle or distribution system allows company X to transport its products/services directly to the consumer through individuals called "distributors" or "independent representatives." In most cases, these individuals are totally responsible for the advertisement, promotion, and selling of the product/services. In this system, the distributors are encouraged in the form of income "bonuses" to recruit, train, and assist other distributors to do the same. Ultimately, the distributor can develop his or her own organization of distributors. Company X pays the distributor commissions, overrides, and bonuses not only for *their* efforts but for the efforts of the others recruited.

Now for the BIG question! Is MLM a "pyramid" scheme where by only the people at the top make money and the people at the bottom are the losers! NO! Absolutely not! MLM is not a pyramid scheme! Read the above comments referencing people at the top making all the money and people at the bottom losing out! Now, you are right to say that in a pyramid system only the people at the top make money and the person at the bottom don't have a chance to ever reach the top! This is a very true definition of "pyramid," however, this definition does not apply to MLM. It is true to your job, civic organization, and everything else. Just think for one moment. I know I just covered this, but it will not kill you to revisit this again. Look at the "pyramid" structure below:

President: the dude (or dudette) at the top

Vice President: the dude next to the dude at the top

Executive Managers: this is the group that blocks everyone else from the top

Mid-level Managers: this group makes a little more money and keeps their thumbs on the supervisors

Supervisors: the most dangerous group. They love telling you what to do, when to do it, and then take the credit for your work.

Employees: the pride of the company. This group does the most work, gets paid the least, and rarely has any opportunity of making it to the top of the pyramid.

Who makes all the money? The guy at the top! What are your chances of getting to the top? Did you say "slim-to-none?" Well 'slim' just walked out of the door and I recommend you do the same. Not really but you better have another plan. In the traditional business, there are limits to your success and income. Look on the back of a one dollar bill. What do you see? There's a pyramid with an eye at the top, which some say represents the capitalists watching over the employees.

Check this out! MLM is a "mathematical system" used to create a continuous flow of cash through "duplication of efforts." MLM deals with numbers. Simply put, the more you are willing to duplicate yourself the more you can earn. My Lord and Savior Jesus Christ used this very same mathematical system! He started with twelve apostles (assistants) and now there are millions of men and women spreading the Gospel. The largest franchises in the history of the United States, 7-Eleven and McDonalds, also use this method. McDonalds has a corporate headquarters, but each restaurant around the world is owned and operated by different owners. The headquarters collects royalties from every owner. This mathematical system is based on the numbers. The more franchises a corporation sets up, the more money it makes! Wow! What a powerful system.

MLM professionals do the exact same thing. They go out and duplicate their business as many times as they can. The more they are willing to set up "franchises" or recruit/sponsor new business partners, the more money they can make! It costs millions of dollars to own and operate a traditional franchise such as Wendy's. First, you have put up the capital to fund the franchise and then attend weeks of training. Next, there are expenses like the building, equipment, inventory, employees, taxes, training, inspections, licenses, and much more. Just think, after seeing to all of that you have not earned one dime. However, at the end of the day most franchise owners are successful because of the duplication process. Mind you, in order to earn a really good income, you must own several franchises! I can speak to this because I am a former franchise owner.

MLM professionals do not have all these headaches. This industry is simple, quick, hassle free, low cost, low overhead, no employees, and you can earn money immediately. Not only can you earn money immediately, there is NO limit to the amount of money you can make! Like your job, right? Not really! You know exactly what you are going to get every week.

Additionally, MLM businesses have all the same tax benefits as the million dollar franchises. You can deduct meals, auto mileage, equipment, computer, stamps, envelopes, entertainment, travel, lodging, parking, and much more. You are already spending money on these items anyway so why not deduct them off your taxes? I am **not** a tax expert or a financial advisor. Make sure you speak to your tax person to learn all the ways you can benefit tax-wise as a multi-level marketing professional.

MLM professionals duplicate themselves all across the country and around the world. Doesn't it make perfect sense to work from home? You are already paying for the house that is completely furnished with chairs, lights, computers, phones, etc.. Your commute is only a minute away! Some days, you sleep in your work clothes and may even sleep with your business partner! You have to be blind *not* to see the benefits of working from home.

The question is: Why do the so called "experts" and government officials say that MLM is an illegal pyramid system? Ignorance! They don't have a clue about what they are talking about! They are merely repeating what other people have passed down through the ages from people who didn't know either. Ever hear the phrase "blind leading the blind?" People are accustomed to listening to others who have little or no experience. I believe that those in "power" are afraid that every American may come to realize that the American dream is still possible and it exists in the form of MLM opportunities. MLM can give you the financial edge you need to help you and your family realize your dream. The only thing the average American needs to achieve that dream is to earn a few more bucks and reduce their tax bill. MLM will give you exactly that and much more. For some reason people don't believe you can actually achieve success using the MLM strategy. My friend, it works and it is working like crazy all around the globe. People need to stop listening to those who have never been involved in MLM. Also, you shouldn't listen to anyone who never gave it a real chance or applied much effort.

I can understand why some people label MLM as a pyramid system or scheme. Let's examine why! When MLM professionals give business presentations about the opportunity and the financial possibilities in this strategy, they normally use a geometrical diagram (draw circles and then draw more circles under those in a 2x2 or 3x3 matrix) that puts the entrepreneur (you) at the top and then draw circles or little people figures under you as your downline & sometime lines to show the connection to your downline and your downlines's downline. In printed materials it looks something like this but just with men figures.

Multi-level Marketing Structure

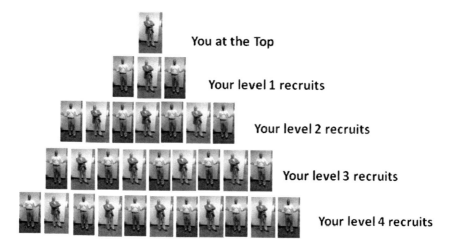

Now, does that look like a pyramid? Of course it does! During the presentation, the presenter put you at the top of the pyramid and shows how your business (and your wealth) can grow as you add more people to your group and then as they duplicate you and add people to their network. This will never work perfectly as demonstrated! It surely didn't work with Jesus and His twelve disciples because one of those guys lost the vision and eventually removed himself from the equation! Additionally, this type of illustration gives the appearance that you are at the top and the others are below you and that these folks are working for you while you sit at the top making all the money. From this poorly-rendered illustration, there has been much confusion, legal battles, and has flat out turned people off from joining. With this type of description, who *wouldn't* think MLM is a pyramid scheme?

Now, the illustration itself isn't too far off; however, it would be more accurate if it was turned upside down! Does it make sense for the newest member of your business to be doing the most work? Nope! You, as the one with the most knowledge and experience, are supporting everyone else above you. You take time to share your knowledge and experience as they grow their business.

Let's Be Honest – You work for them!
Multi-level Marketing Structure

You will do most of the work in the beginning while your team is learning how to grow their business.

The main reason why they show you at the top is because they want you to be the star of show. Everyone like to see themselves at the top of anything they are attempting to do. You get pretty excited when you see the possibilities of earning commissions from the efforts of others. Personally, I didn't think it was possible in the beginning but now I know it does work and if you keep at it for awhile it will take on a life of its' on. And that is exactly what you want to happen.

MLM is not a pyramid structure; it is a mathematical system that cannot be fitted into any kind of structure. MLM is a numbers game. If you sponsor 10 people, 7 will probably quit and never do anything. This is a fact! Why? Because MLM professionals teach their new recruits more about the company and its' products and services than they do on how to succeed in multi-level marketing.

The next time you have to do a business presentation about your MLM opportunity, turn that pyramid upside down so that YOU are at the bottom supporting each new person to the business. You work for them; not the other way around! You don't get paid until they do! Money is passed down to you for helping your new recruit get started. The higher the structure is built, the more money is made and the more support available to each new person. I guess you should call them your "upline" instead of "downline!"

MLM is about building others up. You are to provide motivation, inspiration, training, support, and leadership. In MLM, leadership is an everyday example. It is NOT a Position. This is called the process of duplication.

Hey, you can have both a traditional job and build yourself a MLM/Network Marketing business. Wouldn't it be great to simply earn an additional $2000 to $4000 extra dollars on top of your current salary?

Well you can and you can start right now. Let me ask you a question? Does my buk sound like I am "PRO" MLM/Networking? Well, you are dawg gone right!

Now take a quick look at the Corporate Pyramid Structure below. Not much difference in the design. When you think about it just about every organizational structure form some type of pyramid structure.

Global Recognized Pyramid Structure

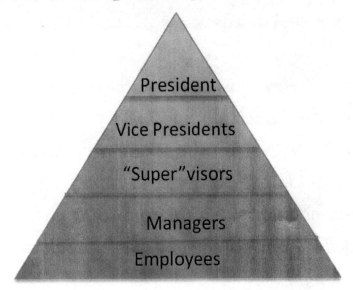

Oh, and while you are checking things out pull out a dollar bill and see what is on the back of your buck!

Your Notes:
Name so other pyramid organizations?

Episode VI

A Divine Beginning

I BELIEVE GOD CREATED EVERYONE TO INCLUDE MLM

There are many people who claim to have created the network marketing industry. Now, for obvious reasons face-to-face communication is how the world functioned for years because there were no telephones, telegraphs, mail, email, etc. In my opinion, the first person to intentionally use network marketing or face-to-face advertising was Jesus Christ. Remember in the Bible He told His disciples to go "two by two" to spread the Gospel (Good News). Well, this is exactly what Jesus did to "advertise" His coming to the world and share all He has done for mankind. So, let it be clear that mankind is where we are today because God loved us so much that He sent His one and only begotten

Son to the Earth to share the Gospel and He did it by word-of-mouth advertisement. God wanted to get the word out with a personal touch. He wanted people to look into the eyes of His disciples and see the truth that they were sharing. God did not want to risk His message being misrepresented. He wanted to make sure that everyone, regardless of status in the community, heard the message and had an opportunity to take full advantage of this heavenly opportunity. The disciples carried God's message all around the world and here we are today still sharing the testimony of Jesus Christ to anyone who will listen. The Gospel is free and affordable to everyone.

It's clear that God laid the foundation for ordinary people to get involved in network marketing to make extraordinary income and to keep people talking one-on-one. Technology is a wonderful thing but when you replace face-to-face communication you miss the most exciting aspect of human interaction. There is nothing like it in the world. People get really excited about meeting new people and having a conversation over a cup of coffee or something. Don't you just flat out enjoy being around friends and family, hugging, kissing, joking, sharing, loving, and watching one another? This type of interaction is one of the highest forms of therapy for the soul. I don't know about you but my soul is electrified when I am around people. Sometimes just walking in a crowd of people simply thrills me. Did you know that the only thing God ever created for mankind was mankind? Everything else God created is for us to fulfill our greatness. In the beginning, God created Adam and Eve and everything else was created for their enjoyment. And, guess what it? It applies to us also.

So, come on, you must admit that God did create everything and word-of-mouth was the only way to pass information and promote events for a very long time. Word-of-mouth was how things were done until someone figured out a way to get paid for advertising! Even today, people are still promoting products, service, events, activities, and other things of interest; however, they are not getting paid for it but you can be! Think about all the things we promote by word-of-mouth and never see a dime in referral fees, but I guarantee someone is getting paid for it.

Now allow me to repeat myself! Today we have so many means to share information including the telephone, texting, Internet, Facebook, Twitter, blogs, newspapers, radio, television, magazines, etc. Still, word-of-mouth is the only form of communication that provides true human interaction, contact, and emotion. No matter what new technology is developed nothing will ever replace face-to-face communication. It is an awesome thing to be able to look someone directly in the eyes and see the essence of life that God breathed into their soul. In fact, we need more face-to-face communication. People today are hiding behind all these devices. You are a lot less apt to tell a lie when speaking directly with a person. Well, not in every case, but for the most part people will say what they believe when you are looking them in their eyes. I do believe you can tell when folks are lying or telling you the truth. We need to get back to the basics of human interaction. We are drifting away from the purpose of life itself and that is being able to touch, smell, hear, and experience another life. Ok, I will save that for another buk! Smile.

So, come on and join the folks who are dreaming again, seeking the best of themselves and seeking the best of others. By participating in MLM, you can join the fastest growing industry in America today.

*Why are you surprised that I am giving Jesus credit for starting the MLM/Networking Marketing industry?
He started everything else.
I have discovered that when you give Jesus the credit and glory for everything, things seems to get better.*

Network Marketing is a beautiful and wonderful opportunity to meet hundreds of people. They are everywhere just waiting for you to walk up to them and share the good news of how they can start their home-based business using this marvelous system called Network Marketing. We make it sounds easy and sometimes it is and sometime it is not. There have been many times I wanted to quit, give up, never speak to another person. If the truth is to be told I have quit on the inside several times but put myself back in the game. There are some very good motivational books out there that will get you excited, pumped up, and roaring to go. See my list of books in the Backups. It is exciting to read positive books and listen to motivational CDs and be around positive people during difficult times and there will be difficult times. Is it worth the frustration? Yes, yes, yes. This is the price we pay to own this type of business. Keep in mind you get some of the same frustrations from your traditional business as well. But you can't quit or take a break from your traditional brick and mortar type business because you have bills to pay. You can pace yourself in a MLM/Network Marketing business. So stick and stay until you get your pay.

Your Notes:
How did you learn about MLM?

Episode VII

Why not a Job?
J-ust O-ver B-roke

A job *will not* allow you to experience the American Dream! Wake up! A job will never be enough. Sure, you can save and invest if you are lucky! However, the truth of the matter is that you will live from paycheck to paycheck until you die. Don't get me wrong, I am not putting jobs down or anything. However, we are discussing the American Dream -- financial freedom and time freedom.

Think about everyone you know. They all constantly complain about not having enough for anything else after they pay the mortgage, car payments, credit card bills, children's educations, and much more. Think about the people who are a generation or two ahead of you. Are any of those folks wealthy? Financially secure? Completely retired? Most likely, they are not! I am willing to bet that the majority of people reading this buk have parents and/or grandparents who are still working. Seriously, those senior citizens working at McDonalds and Wal-Mart have to be someone's parents or grandparents! I will not provide you a lot of statistical information on just how many senior citizens are working after retiring. You can just open your eyes and look around.

I know this is a hard truth to accept, but someone has to tell the truth and say what our parents and other relatives and friends are not willing to admit. I am telling you now why you still have time to start your own business! This country was founded on business ownership. Why do you think the federal government (Internal Revenue Service) offers such great tax benefits and deductions for business owners? The true American Dream is business ownership! When you own a business you have a piece of the pie! You are now in charge of your life! You are the boss and the sky is the limit. Earn as much as you want and deserve. Take a vacation when you want to and not when your boss says you can.

Working a job controls every single thing about your human existence. Who ever controls your paycheck controls you! Your paycheck tells you where you can live, the kind of house you can live in, and the type of furniture you can put in that house. Your paycheck tells you what kind of car you can drive and when you can drive! It controls who your friends are, the food on your table, your vacations, the schools for your children, the medical care you can receive, and the amount of insurance you can have on you and your family. It controls the amount of time you can spend with your family and friends. I hate to say this but it also determines whether or not you can stay home if you or a family member is sick! Your paycheck controls your very existence.

I just don't understand how people can live under these conditions and not try to do something about it! I am not talking about getting rich. I am talking about just making a small difference. Most people are 30 days from filing bankruptcy. All they need is a few extra dollars each month in order to be out from under all the stress of not having enough money. It is one thing not to be able to start a traditional business with brick and mortar that will cost you tens of thousands of dollars. I get that! But what is your excuse for not starting a home business with network marketing? No one in America has a legitimate excuse. Surely you can find $100 to get started. This is all it takes to get started in some kind of business. The problem is that most people have huge ego problems. They have been faking their success so long that they have started believing it themselves. Why? All of your friends and family know the truth. The fact that you live in the same community as they do speaks volumes to your success. I know that material things are not everything and do not define who you are nor what you are going to do with your life. If people would stop spending so much energy in acting like they got it going on and use that energy to do something toward changing their financial suituation they will be better off in the long run. The stupid thing about this is that everybody knows you are broke. Broke doesn't mean you can't pay your bills, but it means that *after* you pay your bills you can't buy anything else.

So what are you going to do? Continue to work your 9-to-5 job and hope and pray you don't get laid off? Or, are you going to get off your duff and get busy? The MLM industry is a very positive and upbeat industry. We have a ton of fun and meet some of the most wonderful people on the planet. In this industry, people believe in you and will help you reach your highest level of success.

> Did you know that most heart attacks occur on Monday mornings?
> It is said that people hate their jobs so bad that they would rather die than to spend another day on the job. You may want to start your week on Tuesdays.

I think I should write a little bit more because I don't want you to leave you with that last thought. Just try and understand that your job does not have to be the final say to your financial future. Just start a MLM business and earn a few extra bucks on top of what you are already earning from your job and you will be surprised at what you can do. Hey, you can even change your zip code and make some new friends and God knows we all can use some new friends, right. That's better! Talk to you in the next Episode. It will have a different title and I will repeat some stuff so you will get the point. Be patient and read.

Your Notes:
What do you like and dislike about your job?

_____
_____
_____
_____
_____
_____
_____
_____
_____
_____
_____
_____
_____
_____
_____
_____

"Things you need to know before launching your MLM home business"

Episode VIII

Why not a Traditional Business?
THE AVERAGE PERSON CAN'T AFFORD IT

If you have ever looked into starting a traditional "store front", you would find out that it costs thousands of dollars to get started. You must lease office space, purchase office furniture and equipment, and establish an inventory. We can't forget about the headache that comes with employees such as unemployment compensation, insurance, and other tax withholdings. That is just the beginning! Then there is this statistic: More than 50 percent of new businesses fail within the first five years. Friends, the odds are against you before you open your door. Don't get me wrong, I love traditional brick and mortar businesses. However, they are costly to start and very few people who want to own a business can actually afford to do so.

On the other hand, MLM is a very low cost business to start with minimal risk. You can start a MLM business for less than the cost of a soft drink a day. In most cases, you do not have the traditional headaches that come with a new business. You are the boss! When you wake up in the morning you are either the "boss" or the "employee". You can work as hard or as easy as you want to. Your overhead is your home! You already pay the mortgage and utilities and you probably have a few family members at home that could be considered employees! There are MLM businesses you can join for less than $100. Yes, $100! Hey, most people blow $100 on junk food! If you are working a job and don't have $100 to start a MLM business, you need to close this book and find someone in a MLM business to help you get started right away.

The average person spends the majority of their life living in a "RUT." What is a RUT? A

RUT is process in which you do the same thing over and over again and expecting "NEW" results without doing something differently. You get up every morning at the same time to go to the same job and do the same work then leave to come home to sit in the same spot and later go to bed and start the next day doing the same things again. Before you know, it years and years have passed and all of your dreams and goals were pushed to the back burner so that you could spend your precious time at a job helping someone else achieve their dreams and goals for their family. Oooops....that hurts! Wow, you spent your entire life building someone else's dreams and goals and you neglected yours and your family's goals.

I know you don't have time to start a home biz, right?

We all have enough time! There are no 9-to-5 jobs these days; they went away many years ago! In today's economy, you work from sun up to sun down! You spend hours in traffic getting to and from work. Your weekends are getting shorter and shorter! Between cutting the lawn, cleaning out the garage, fixing things around the house, church on Sundays, and then a couple of hours with the family, you don't have any time left. Does this cover your life pretty much? The question is how do you manage a business when you have so little time? You probably feel that you don't have enough time right now to start a MLM, but you DO! Stop using that as an excuse!

MLM is a business that does not just pay you based on what you do alone, but it pays you on what you start. You get paid not only from your efforts but also from the efforts of hundreds, maybe thousands of others-- people who are giving a little bit of time toward their

MLM business just like you. By everyone giving up a little bit of time, you earn thousands of dollars from the efforts of others. It is not about how much or how little time you have! It is about showing others that by working as a team "together, everyone achieves more!" You can achieve your dream!

Will you get rich over night? No! If anyone ever tells you that, run from them as fast as you can. <u>Start slow! Get your family involved.</u> Set a few goals. Then, put in as much time as you can. Give up a little TV. Give up a little golf. Give up a few lunch hours and a few bowling nights. You have time. Stop making excuses. Stop looking for reasons why you *can't* do it and look for reasons why you can and should. Look in the face of your spouse and your kids. Don't they deserve the best things in life? This life is not a rehearsal. It is the only one you have. Make sure you are right with God and allow God to bless your life so that you can be a blessing to someone. Don't you want to have enough, even an overflow, so that you can have something to share with others who truly don't have the physical and mental capacity to do it for themselves? Don't you think your Pastor would deeply appreciate you having more so that you can give more to the church? I think the church could do more with 10% of $100,000 than they can with 10% of $50,000. It is not always about you! Even the Bible speaks about the importance of giving to others, feeding others, serving others, helping others, and loving others. Not to mention your family would truly appreciate you providing them with the opportunity to make different choices and/or more choices. For example, maybe your family would like to ski in Europe instead of West Virginia. Or, maybe your wife would like to shop at Macy's instead of Wal Mart. There is nothing wrong with skiing in West Virginia or shopping at Wal Mart. It is about having choices and giving other's choices.

The truth of the matter is that the all mighty dollar provides choices no matter who you are, your color, race, religion, sex, etc.. If you have dollars, you have choices.

Your Notes:
List the things you don't like about traditional biz

_____
_____
_____
_____
_____
_____
_____
_____
_____
_____
_____
_____
_____
_____
_____

Episode IX

Can You Really Earn Money in MLM?
YES YOU CAN BUT IT WILL TAKE SOME SWEAT EQUITY

Yes! Yes! Yes! I wouldn't be pouring out my heart to you about starting a MLM home business if it were not possible to earn money doing so! You can earn a few dollars or you can earn hundreds, thousands, and in some cases, millions of dollars. MLM is not a get-rich-quick scheme. Allow me to apologize to you for those individuals who promote this industry as a way you can get rich overnight. Let's be real! The probability of getting rich in MLM is remote. You have a better chance of getting struck by lightening three times on the same day. While you may not get rich in MLM it IS possible to obtain wealth! Owning a MLM business provides an additional income stream to supplement your current income, which gives you the extra funds you need to pay off debt, take vacations, or just spend time as you WANT to spend it instead of how a job dictates you spend it. You can also use your extra funds to invest and build up wealth. Owning your own business allows you to take advantage of the great tax deductions that come along with business ownership. Your MLM business also provides you access to a network of highly motivated group of people all striving to achieve financial independence. Combine all these advantages together and you have a formula for wealth. You can achieve this wealth working part time or in your spare time. For those of you already in MLM, stop selling a pipe dream to your friends and family. The truth of the matter is that only a few individuals actually earn millions of dollars in this industry. I would venture to say that only one out of one hundred thousand representatives in a company will earn a million dollars within five- to-ten years with a MLM company. Can you replace your existing income with a MLM home business? Yes, you can! However, I recommend that you first get out of debt. Next, save up at least one year of your annual income and set that in the bank as a back up. Then, wait until you have at least doubled or tripled your current income with your MLM home business for three years. Otherwise, don't quit your day job. Again, your MLM home business is to supplement your job's income!

I expect a lot of MLM home business owners are going to be very upset with me for letting the "cat out of the bag." Well, we have the greatest opportunity in the world! God has blessed us with an opportunity that can change the lives of millions of people. If we continue sugar coating the reality of having an MLM business, many people will miss out because of all the "hype." Stop! Stop! Stop, feeding people all this hype! Everyone can not and will not make a million dollars a year. Can it be done and are there people doing it? YES! But, the truth is most people will only earn a few extra hundred or maybe a thousand dollars a month. A few extra thousand dollars a month may seem like million dollars to some. However, as I mentioned before, all you need is a few more bucks a month to make a huge difference in your quality of life.

See Top 25 – 150 listed in Worldwide Earners in MLM – April 2014 in Backup.

> You will never know what you
> are capable of until you
> get away from in front of the
> TV and do something.
> Stop watching others succeed and
> start working toward your own success.

Your Notes:
What are you going to buy with your first check?

I'm not going to spend it. I will use it to open another bank account to deposit all my checks so I can see my business progress.

Episode X

What about Tax Benefits?

LOTS OF TAX BENEFITS BUT GET PROFESSIONAL ADVISE

Let me begin by saying that I am not a certified tax consultant, preparer, accountant, nor a tax expert. The small amount of information I know about tax benefits should be confirmed with your accountant or the Internal Revenue Service. Now to answer the question: Yes, every individual in the United States should be taking advantage of all the tax benefits available through business ownership.

This is probably the best kept secret in America and it is a crying shame that people work hard day in and day out to earn an income only to turn around and give a big chunk of it back to the government. I have no problems with the government taxing the people to help run the government. What I do have a problem with is the fact that Americans pay millions of dollars in taxes that should be returned to people like you, but are not. You must position yourself in a way to take legitimate tax deductions so that you do not have to pay more taxes than you owe. Get smart about it.

Most Americans are either too lazy or just scared of the IRS and thus just pay their taxes without asking questions. The Internal Revenue Service is run by human beings—people just like you and me. Contrary to popular opinion, the people in the IRS do not have two heads and breathe fire! I have found them to be extremely helpful and understanding of your tax concerns. They will do everything they can to help you and explain all your rights as a tax payer.

I will never forget the first time I was audited by the IRS. I was scared to death! I thought the government had people who were following me around. Everyday I found myself looking out the windows for government cars parked in front of my house. I was a nervous wreck! Then, audit day arrived. I had to report to the IRS office with all my paper work to support my tax return. The lady could tell right away that I was scared and very uncomfortable. It may have been the sweat running down my face that gave me away! It was quite an experience. She helped me calm down and it all went very smoothly from there. She explained to me that I was "red flagged" in the system because of an increase noted in my deductions used in "Schedule C." I will not try to explain what a "Schedule C" is; however, your tax accountant should be able to. If not, find another tax accountant right away. Anyway, the audit went very smoothly. I had everything in order and the IRS was very satisfied with my documentation! My tax accountant had done a very good job preparing my taxes and ensuring I had all the proper supporting documentation to support my return. The IRS is not out to get you! Matter of fact, the IRS agent assisted me by giving me some ideas on how to keep track of the deductions I could use if I would keep the receipts.

Since that time I have been audited several other times for different reasons. The most recent two times were surrounding a tremendous increase in my income and large charitable contributions. Now, when you get audited because you made a lot more money than the year before, you should be smiling all the way to the bank! Additionally, to be audited for giving a lot of money to your church through tithes and offerings is also a good thing! The amazing thing I found out was that people who make over a million dollars a year do not tithe as much as I do. The IRS agent stated that it is rare for people to give over $10,000 a year in charitable contributions. I was shocked to find out that there are people making millions of dollars who do not give at least $10,000 or more to their church.

Your MLM home business offers you all the same tax benefits of any other traditional business. Let's take a look at some of the possible tax deductions.

If you establish a home office to run your business, here are some of the tax deduction possibilities: Put a check by the things you have and are not currently deducting them from your taxes:

____ Office furniture
✓ Computers
____ Fax machines
____ Copier
✓ Office Telephones
✓ Cell phone
✓ Internet service

_____ Office stationary
_____ Stamps & Envelopes
__✓__ Planners
__✓__ Pens & Pencils
_____ Software
_____ Audio and video equipment
_____ Overhead projector
__✓__ Meals
__✓__ Meeting expenses
__✓__ Seminars
__✓__ Training
__✓__ Lodging/Hotel rooms
_____ Entertainment
_____ Ads
__✓__ Flyers
__✓__ Gas mileage
_____ Parking
_____ Tolls
__✓__ Business Cards   ✓ hot spot
_____ Vacations
_____ Clothes with business logos and much more.

As long as these items are conducted in conjuction with your business, you may be able to deduct all or part of these items. You are going to spend money in most of these areas anyway, therefore, why not take a few bucks and invest it in a MLM home business? It just makes sense! <u>The first step in learning how to make money is to learn how to save the money you are already earning.</u> Starting a MLM home business is the first step toward learning how to save money. If you refuse to start a MLM home business because you think you are too good, you have a super ego, you have a lot of education, what others will think, old school pride, or any other stupid reason, you deserve to be broke.

One of the first things you need to learn about making money is learning how to keep it.

You can truly enjoy a great part time income. Later, I will share about the myths of MLM as far as getting rich over night. MLM is not designed to make you rich even if there are several documented examples of people who have. They are the exception to the rule and for the most part, you probably will only meet one or two people who achieve that luxury. So, don't get into this type of business with the mindset of getting rich! The truth of the matter is you probably will not! Now, I will probably get a lot of criticism about this, however, the truth must be told. Most small business owners will not become rich. You can become financially secure. From there, you can have greater control over your life and its circumstances. By earning additional income and taking advantage of all the tax benefits self-ownership allows, you will begin to see a lifestyle change. You will begin to make every dollar count and be wise with your spending. The best part is when you start thinking like a business owner and begin to understand some of the financial strategies available to you. So, call that person who offered you a business opportuntiy and start taking advantage of the tax benefits. Please remember to consult a certified tax preparer or tax consultant. You can find out most things on the Internet so make sure to do your research.

Your Notes:
What tax deduction do you have now?

computer
copies
gas
vehicle repair
cell phone
internet
meeting
timeshare usage
simulcast
hotel meeting cost
magazines
sign up fee
monthly website upkeep

Episode XI

Is This a Family Business?

YES! DADS, MOMS, BROTHERS, SISTERS, AUNTS, UNCLES MAKE MONEY WITH YOUR FRIENDS AND FRIENDS WITH YOUR MONEY

Again, yes! You normally operate this type of business from home and it is something you and your family can do together. In fact, I highly recommend you get them involved. You will find out that you will get a lot more support if your family is involved. Families that do operate their business together have a tremendous amount of success in the MLM industry. You can travel together and even take business vacations together. Your children will grow from being around entrepreneurs who are positive, upbeat, motivated, and live life with a purpose.

My son truly enjoyed traveling to meetings and seminars with me. He received a lot of attention from other business owners and was able to meet people from all walks of life. He saw his father interacting with other positive people. This positive attitude flowed over into his school work and his relationships with his peers. Today, he believes he can do anything if he puts his mind to it. My son sees his father out there doing his utmost for his family instead of sitting around complaining about not being able to provide for them. Remember, your family will eventually judge you on what you do and not what you say. Are you setting the right example? It is amazing how many people work all week to make someone else rich, but they do not take a few extra hours a week to start something for them and their families. You know, our children didn't ask to come into this world. Nor do they have a choice who their parents are. They are stuck with you and you are pretty much all they have to depend on to set the best example. What example are you giving them?

My wife enjoys the socialization that comes with being in this business. She especially enjoys meeting other women and sharing ideas on how to grow their businesses. They get very excited about the new things they plan to buy with the additional income, the vacations they can take, and the opportunity to help other family members. Many women succeed in MLM businesses because they are natural speakers able to communicate well with others and enjoy earning money while working from home and raising a family.

Is MLM a Cult or Revival?

Well, what's your definition of a cult and a revival? According to the dictionary, a cult is: 1. formal religious veneration: worship; 2: a system of religious beliefs and ritual; 3: a great devotion to a person, idea, or thing. A revival is defined as: 1: an act or instance of reviving: the state of being revived: as a: renewed attention to or interest in something b: a new presentation or publication, c: a period of renewed religious interest. 2: an often highly emotional evangelistic meeting or series of meetings.

The short answer to the question is no, but pretty darn close! There is absolutely nothing wrong with being excited about anything in life. We have labels for everything and everyone. There are good labels and bad labels. Some labels are very accurate and true and others are very wrong and not true. Who comes up with these labels? We all do and labels play a major role in our society so don't get blown away with people saying that MLM is a Cult or Revival of some sort. And even if it fits the definition to a tee it is not a bad thing. When you attend a football, basketball, baseball, or soccer game, you see all these people yelling and screaming, but you don't think they are in a "Cult or in a Revival." No, they are not and again, there is nothing to say that a Cult or Revival is a bad event, activity or gathering. When someone or some group that is a part of a larger group hurts us on purpose or simply makes a mistake we tend to put a negative label on the entire organization. This is all part of life and MLM is not immune to negative labels. When you attend a major MLM conference you will find that people are highly motivated, they yell, they scream, and have lots of fun just as they do at sporting events, church activities, music concerts, just to name few. Believe it or not, there is no alcohol involved. Yes, people can have big fun without any help and they remember the fun to boot! If the truth is to be told, I love the heck out these MLM rallys and conferences as I do sporting events and church revivals. I love the excitement! I believe this world would be a lot better off if we all were more positive, upbeat and excited about life and about helping others. So don't be shocked when you walk into a local meeting or an arena and someone you do not know gives you a big hug. MLMers will one day bring the entire world together because we believe in the American Dream, we believe in each other, and we believe in you. We are willing to work with a perfect stranger and help them achieve their dreams and goals. When was the last time a family member or friend walked up to you and said "how would you like to earn some additional income and get rid of your debt"? I will answer for you, never. And yes we hug perfect strangers so come on board and get yours.

Your Notes:
Who are you going to invite to your first presentation?

Episode XII

Is it Difficult to Work a MLM Business?

THE ONLY PLACE WHERE SUCCESS COMES BEFORE WORK IS IN THE DICTIONARY

Yes, work is hard and owning your own MLM business is work. However, it is a very simple business to start. With a reputable MLM business, you will receive great support and training. In most cases, you will have a sponsor who has a financial interest in your success and who is therefore ready to help you start your business. While this will be your own business, you will definitely not be in it by yourself! This is one of the great thing about MLM: you can and will get plenty of help.

When you first start your MLM business you obviously will not know everything about the company. You probably saw the presentation of what the opportunity offers and were intrigued enough to become involved. The product/service is good, the cost to join was affordable for you, the concept appeared to be simple, and you know a lot of people.

Once you are signed up, you have to start working it! Again, you will receive a lot of training and your upline will have the knowledge and willingess to help you launch your business. Most companies will also have some kind of training available on their websites. That training is usually centered around the company and its products and/or services. Many companies, though, do not really provide MLM training—that is, training on how to successfully operate a multilevel marketing business that involves goal setting, networking, relationship building, presentation delivery, and all the details associated with building a strong foundation from which your business can grow.

With that being said most of the new start up companies are getting on board and have begun developing MLM training. There are also hundreds of experienced MLM business owners who provide training opportunities and tools that will help you grow your business. If your company doesn't provide training or resources on how to conduct a MLM business, you need to talk to those who are in the business and learn from them!

Now let's talk about the hardest thing about MLM. Simply put, it's people. Yep, people! They will drive you absolutely nuts! In fact, you will get a huge lesson about people-- especially those closest to you! MLM is about you being able to build a network of people who, if given the opportunity to do so, will build a very successful home business to generate additional income. What you will find is that it is fairly easy to get people to sign up to start a business, but it is like pulling teeth to get them working that business at times. Everyone desires to have additional income. They would love to have a new car, a bigger home, take a nice a vacation, earn extra money to send their kids to college, or simply pay off a few bills. Just about everyone you meet will tell you they need more money. But the big problem is most people will not do a thing about it. People will sign up to start a home business, but then they will do absolutely nothing with it. Some will try it for a few days or a few weeks, but most fall back to their normal routine and act as if they never signed up. They quickly forget about their "why" and they will also quickly forget about you. I am laughing right now because this is just amazing to me. Here you are willing to do whatever it takes to help a new business partner and they will not return your phone calls or respond to your emails.

You probably would like to know why, right? Well, there are many reasons why and it will take too much time to explain them all, but I will share with you one of the biggest reasons. The sponsor will make the business opportunity sound so good and easy that everyone who hears the presentation will want to join. The sponsor will then encourage the new partner to get started right away. The sponsor never tells the new business partner how negative their family and friends can be and that they should not go and talk to them alone. So the new business owner rushes over to the home of a friend or family member to share their excitement about starting a new business. Have you heard the expression, "Someone popped his bubble?" This is exactly what happens to new business partners. Friends and family members can be very insensitive and even down right cold hearted. They can be very negative when it comes to talking about money or when you ask them for their support. While I know this is not true with all family members and friends, please be mindful that I am not talking about the exception to the rule. I am talking about the rule. Close family members and friends can and will steal your dreams and goals from you. They may not mean you any harm or desire to hurt you, but they will tell you all the reasons why NOT to take this new opportunity rather than support and encourage you in doing so.

Where can I find information on MLM?

There are many websites that offer information on how to be successful in this industry! Several books have been written about MLM and there will be many more. Years ago, none of this information was available. The MLM industry has received a very negative review from the media and the federal government. Just like any other industry, we police our industry for those few who make it bad for everyone. MLM works and it is here to stay. For those of you who are bold enough to give it a try you will be glad you did.

Your Notes:
Why should you start your MLM Business?

Episode XIII

Who are Owners of MLM Businesses?
TOM, DICK, & HARRY

Someone in every occupation on the planet is involved in this exciting industry. We have everyone from your stay at home mom and/or dad to corporate lawyers. That's right! Everyone with a title, office parking space, corner office, and key to the men's room is making money in MLM. We have doctors, lawyers, ministers, congressmen, mayors, and other politicians involved. Most of these folks are broke but at a different lifestyle level. Many people are credit card rich, living paycheck to paycheck and are one paycheck away from being homeless. They may act as if they do not need money, but they do. Being in debt and in need of money is a very hard thing to admit. This is one of the reasons why it is so hard for "professionals" to come to a hotel meeting to view a business presentation. They are afraid of whom they may see at the meeting. Look, when you drive a fancy car, live in an expensive community, and your kids are in private school, you can't be caught at a MLM meeting learning how to earn additional income. We all have egos and a certain level of pride. I know I do! Being poor is not an easy thing to admit and most people don't. They would rather continue to fake it instead of doing something to make it. So, if you find it difficult to get your professional friends and family members to a meeting this is why. The good news is that more and more people are getting over their pride and passed their egos and are really looking at MLM as a strong avenue to generate revenue. If you know of a professional that is in a MLM business try to get them to do a one-on-one presentation with that friend. I truly believe in the years to come more and more professionals will be getting involved in this industry because it is very lucrative. The beauty of this industry is that it does not discriminate against anyone! You can be 18 or 80, crippled or crazy, married, single or separated, and you can start a MLM business today and become very successful.

Why so many people are starting a MLM home business? Good question! Simply because of the following:

- Great Tax Benefits
- Low cost & low risk
- Unlimited income potential
- No educational requirements
- Great products & service
- Anyone can do it
- BIG fun
- Exciting
- Meet lots of people from around the country and world
- Everyone should own a business – this is the American Dream

- It is legal, ethical, and moral
- Lots of help, training, and support
- You are in it for yourself but not by yourself
- It makes DOLLARS & SENSE and I am just being HONEST

You can have a GED or PHD; graduated from Yale or just got out of Jail. It doesn't matter about your educational background, sex, race, religion, or where you come from. The MLM industry is changing lives everywhere.

The MLM industry is going to explode and people from all over the world are going to join this amazing industry because where else can you start a home business and potentially earn an unlimited income while changing your life forever? The question of the day is: do you believe enough in yourself to start a MLM business today?

Your Notes:
Who do you know that is building a MLM business?

Recommendations

Start a home base MLM business today and become a MLM/Network Marketing Professional. You will be glad you did.

Epic

Thank You

OK, I am done with this buk! Thanks for spending an hour of your time with me! I hope you got what you were hoping for. If not, read it again! By the way here is a BIG MLM HUG from me. I love you and God loves you too.

Acknowledgments

To My God:

I would like to first give thanks to my Lord and Savior Jesus Christ for His love, mercy, and grace. Without Him I can do nothing; and, with Him I can do all things. All Glory, Praise, and Honor to Him and Him alone.

To my immediate family:

I cannot thank my beautiful, warm, and loving wife Franchestee J. Barner enough for her untiring devotion and support throughout our 34 years of marriage, my 20 years of military service, and my 38 years in the MLM/Networking Marketing industry. Fran, you are the reason why I desire to wake up every day of my life.

Special thanks go to my awesome son Haven for allowing me to drag him along on all of my one-on-one appointments and evening business presentations. Son, the day you were born I was overwhelmed with pride and it is a feeling that continues today as I watch the young man you are becoming. Congratulations on your appointment to the United States Military Academy, West Point. I am so proud of you.

To my beautiful and cheerful daughter Gabriella, who keeps Fran and I extremely busy with gymnastics, dance, church choir, music lessons, swimming, and at least 10 sleepovers each month, you keep us young and all our dreams alive.

To HL's family:

Special thanks to my mom, Alice, who gave me life, love, comfort, and taught us the meaning of family. Mom, you will always be the apple of my eye and every beat of my heart. To my brothers and sisters who made life interesting, challenging, and exciting: George the eldest & his wonderful wife Barbara, you both are the guiding light of our family. Earl (deceased), Ricky, Cyrus, Peter, Holly, Linda, Cynthia, Alford, Bobby, Beebe & her husband Noel, Maurice, & Angela. You are the best siblings anyone could ever ask for. I thank God for each of you. That's right, my mom built the first downline in our family! Oh yeah, hi to all my nieces, nephews, and cousins.

To my two aunts Chris White & Shirley Christians who loved me, sheltered me, fed me, encouraged, believed in me, disciplined me, and have always been there for me, I love you both. When you have two super aunts like you guys how could I go wrong. I would have never made it without your hands on my life.

To my uncle Dr. Luther White who has been the inspirational messanger at all our family reunions: Mr. "You can do it", "Just Work at it", "Don't give up "Just hang in there", or "Don't worry about it just try it again". I will always cherish your strong grips & powerful hugs.

To my wife's family:

So many thanks must also go to my amazing mother-in-law Ruth Maria McNair who is my number one fan, supporter, business partner, customer, cheerleader, prayer warrior, motivator, and counselor. You have been such an inspiration to me over the years. I have learned so much from you. You are "Super Fantastic". Congratulations on your 80th birthday!

And to my father-in-law Samuel McNair who is the head this clan. I thank you for being an example of a true servant of God, a friend when I needed one, and a father to all of us. Always willing to give selflessly of time and resources. Thank you so very much.

To my brothers-in-law Colonel Fritzgerald McNair and Cedric Power: You both have made life for me and my family absolutely wonderful. Your love, support, dependability, encouragement, and dedication have earned you the right to be addressed as just "my brothers." To have two strong Christian men as examples for my children is priceless. You guys are awesome.

To my sisters-in-law Verita and Flo: You both are amazing and I don't know what Fran and I would have done without you when we needed your support. You have always been there no matter the need. You both make the holidays a blast and you never forget a birthday. As God- fearing women and aunts to our children, you have had a positive impact on them. Thank you so much for all you do.

To my nieces Cassidy and Faith and my nephew Jonathan, I am so excited to see what life brings you guys. You all are blessed to have fantastic parents and a host of loving relatives to guide you through life. I love each of you and am proud to be your uncle.

To my first MLM Family:

I offer my most sincere thanks to the young man who first introduced network marketing to me. I don't recall his name, but he was in the Air Force and serving at Langley Air Force Base when he truly changed my life.

I must also thank an absolutely wonderful couple who signed me up in my first network marketing business and became my first sponsors: Hector and Rose New. Another special thanks goes to my upline: Betty & Mac and Randolph & Jenny Church and friend Steward (deceased).

Thanks to the greatest country in the world that offers every citizen the opportunity to live a fulfilled life if only they pursue the American dream. That dream is the right to fail as well as succeed; and, the opportunity to live free, freely live, serve, and honor those who serve.

Thanks to you, the reader, who may be interested in joining this industry, but first want to learn the basic truth of multi-level marketing.

Finally, to my fellow networkers who are developing their knowledge of this great and powerful financial vehicle and want to use this industry to change their finacial situation: good luck and best wishes. It is a fantastic journey!

To my executive assistant and editor of my first "buk" Jennifer Bays, you have been my guiding light and inspiration to complete this buk. It has been a very long journey and the completion of this buk is soley due to your belief in me and dedication to seeing it get done. You are God-sent and I look forward to working with you on all my future projects. Thanks for not giving up on me and standing by me through the completion of this buk.

Backup

10 of MY FAVORITE BOOKS:

Book Name	Author
1. The Holy Bible	God
2. God's Big Ideal	Myles Munroe
3. GO PRO	Eric Worre
4. Your First Year of Network Marketing	Mark Yarnell
5. The Magic of Thinking Big	David Schwartz
6. The Greatest Salesman in the World	Og Mandino
7. See you at the Top	Zig Ziglar
8. Enthusiasm Makes the Difference	Dr. Peale
9. MLM Magic	Venus Adrechy
10. The Millionaire Next Door	Stanley/Danko

Top 25 of 150 Worldwide Earners

In MLM - April 2014

by TED NUYTEN on APRIL 20, 2014 (http://www.businessforhome.org/)

The ranking The estimated earnings are based on Internet research, earnings claims from conventions, downline, upline, crossline information, direct selling magazines and through our 70+ reporters.

Numerous top earners and companies share earnings with us. Our objective is to show people, you can make an honest living with MLM, Direct Selling working with all kind of Direct Selling Companies.

These leaders had an incredible vision, empower people, and change their life through this business. They build Million-Dollar

Distributorships through Million Dollar Relationships.

WW Rank	Name	Company	Est. Month	Est. Year	Website
1	Dexter & Birdie Yager	Amway	$1,300,000	$15,600,000	www.dexandbirdieyager.com
2	Holton Buggs	OrganoGold	$1,200,000	$14,400,000	www.organogold.com
3	Angela Liew and Ryan Ho	NuSkin	$1,100,000	$13,200,000	www.nuskin.com
4	Shane Morand	OrganoGold	$1,000,000	$12,000,000	www.organogold.com
5	Barry Chi & Holly Chen	Amway	$650,000	$7,800,000	www.amway.com
6	Brian McClure	Ambit	$452,000	$5,424,000	www.ambitenergy.com
7	Foo Howe Kean & Jenny Ko	Amway	$450,000	$5,400,000	www.amway.com
8	Jose Ardon	OrganoGold	$450,000	$5,400,000	www.organogold.com
9	David Wood and David Sharpe	Empower Network	$400,000	$4,800,000	www.empowernetwork.com
10	George Zalucki & Art Napolitano	ACN	$400,000	$4,800,000	www.georgezalucki.com
11	Sunny Hsu & Debra Hsieh	Amway	$400,000	$4,800,000	www.envip.com/en.asp
12	Tom & Bethany Alkazin	Vemma	$400,000	$4,800,000	www.vemma.com
13	Abraham Benitez and Raquel Cortez	Herbalife	$395,000	$4,740,000	www.herbalife.com
14	Enrique and Graciela Varela	Herbalife	$395,000	$4,740,000	www.herbalife.com
15	Steve Thompson	Ambit	$370,000	$4,440,000	www.rsthompson.com
16	Christian Steinkeller	OrganoGold	$360,000	$4,320,000	www.world.organogold.com
17	Carol & Ken Porter	Monavie	$350,000	$4,200,000	www.Monavie.com

WW Rank	Name	Company	Est. Month	Est. Year	Website
18	John Sachtouras	OrganoGold	$350,000	$4,200,000	www.organogold.com
19	Jonathan Mendoza	Lucrazon	$350,000	$4,200,000	www.latinoecommercesolutions.com
20	Nancy Dornan	Amway	$350,000	$4,200,000	www.n21corp.com
21	Tae Ho Kim	Herbalife	$350,000	$4,200,000	www.herbalife.com
22	Philip Eckart	Ambit	$324,000	$3,888,000	www.ambitenergy.com
23	Carol and Alan Lorrenz	Herbalife	$300,000	$3,600,000	www.herbalife.com
24	Kaoru Nakajima	Amway	$300,000	$3,600,000	www.heckel.ne.jp
25	Simon Abboud	ACN	$300,000	$3,600,000	www.ACNinc.com

About the Author

Dr. H. L. Barner started his Network Marketing career over 38 years ago and has become one of the premier Multi-Level Marketing team builders in the world today. He has been a top income earner with several MLM companies. His downline organizations expanded the borders of the United States into Canada, Germany, and England. He is one of the most entertaining, motivational and inspirational speaker trainers in the history of Network Marketing. He has a vast amount of knowledge about the Network Marketing industry. He has created several marketing systems and training techniques that are being used throughout the Network Marketing industry. Dr. H. L. Barner tell you like it is, make plain and simple. When you attend one of trainings you walk out filled with ideas, confidence and a new attitude towards your MLM/Network Marketing business.

CPSIA information can be obtained at www.ICGtesting.com
Printed in the USA
BVOW03s1615011014

369095BV00006B/11/P